The
AMERICAN
DREAM
after retirement

PALMETTO
PUBLISHING
Charleston, SC
www.PalmettoPublishing.com

Copyright © 2024 by Ronald F. Whalen

All rights reserved
No portion of this book may be reproduced, stored in a retrieval system, or transmitted in any form by any means–electronic, mechanical, photocopy, recording, or other–except for brief quotations in printed reviews, without prior permission of the author.

Paperback ISBN: 9798822963139

RONALD F. WHALEN

The
AMERICAN DREAM
after retirement

A step-by-step guide to
success for attaining your
American Dream

No special skills necessary, just "Dream Big, Never Quit" - success is waiting for you to begin.

CHAPTER 1:

A belief in The American Dream has been with all of us since this bountiful country began. People from countries all around the world who migrate to the United States have a picture - a vision - in their minds of The American Dream and hope (dream) they can attain it. They are very willing to leave their native countries to come to America to start a better way of life, and along the way discover The American Dream that brought them here to America.

American citizens, especially those born in the United States tend to grow up in a lifestyle envied by so many who hope to migrate here and become American citizens themselves one day. Still, with all that we American citizens have in this country, life can be very difficult for many different reasons. Throughout their lives, the vision of a much better, more successful life still resides within them, vision of their American Dream!

Even those of us who led a relatively good life find, after retirement, an emptiness, a less satisfying life than we had when younger and employed. We dream of something better, something more satisfying for our remaining time. For most people the vision returns! A vision of achieving something special in the time we have left. That "something special" is securing The American Dream!

Well, I did it, and so can you! Continue reading and start achieving your AmericanDream; it's waiting for you.

CHAPTER 2:
My story:

I retired at the age of 76 following a lifetime of working in several different disciplines, including Information Technology, private security, and teaching at several universities and technical schools. Prior to my numerous career endeavors, a six-year enlistment in the United States Marine Corps taught me discipline, training, and the spirit of not giving up.

Over the years I earned a relatively good education in different subjects. First, I earned my BA in Business Operations, then my MS in Criminal Justice. Following that, I went back to school and earned my Ph.D. in Business Management. My education, however, did not play a role in choosing my American Dream! Once retired, I was free from serving large corporations to earn a living, free from the rules and regulations of teaching, and I no longer answered to others for my salary. My retirement allowed me the freedom to dream; to decide for myself what I wanted to do, what direction the rest of my life would take. Now, your education may benefit you once you know your dream, but recognizing your American Dream is totally up to you.

I tell people my retirement lasted approximately four hours, spent sitting on my sofa and watching TV. Of course, it lasted a bit longer than that. However, I did realize very early on that sitting around the house with idle time was not for me. This was not the retirement life I wanted! I wanted to go on but had no idea how to do so. I volunteered with several community-related agencies and tried several activities to keep busy and pass the time.

Fortunately, my health was good, and my mind was still working well enough for a person in their 70's. This allowed me the freedom to explore various ideas and determine what my American Dream was to become. I wanted to build something; create something that did not exist. But, where to start?

Well, I discovered I really enjoyed the challenge of golf, and after a while I started to dream of how I could improve the game. Just about everything and anything related to this enormous industry was already created, produced, and engaged in the marketing of golf products. I wanted to get involved in something unique to the game but could not come up with anything new --- until I saw a company advertising a "zero friction" golf tee. Knowing it was impossible to achieve zero friction from a golf tee, I started dreaming of ways to accomplish a product that would be close. When we dream, we can create anything!!! I began to envision a golf ball floating on a layer of air above the golf tee --- that's it, I told myself – Zero Friction!

I spent a lot of quality time on my computer, researching existing golf tees and their effects on the golf balls as they are hit and leave the surface of the tee. What could I design to make the flight of the golf ball better?

I began drawing my ideas on paper, then called my son Daniel, who is an excellent engineer and great golfer. I told him of my plans to create a golf ball tee that can "float" a golf ball, and instead of telling me it was impossible, he immediately offered to help me with the specific design parameters and information necessary to create this product. Together we designed a golf tee which contained a tiny but powerful motor / battery system that channeled air up through the top of the tee, providing an "almost" "zero-friction" golf tee.

After several attempts, we actually built a working prototype! Were we successful in building a unique zero friction-like golf tee? YES. However, were we successful in building a

3

product that anyone would even consider buying and using on a golf course? NO! Was this a time to quit? Absolutely NO! Rationality began to settle in, and we realized we had the right concept, but the wrong product. Back to the drawing board. What we needed to do was re-design our golf tee to become a "performance tee"; no motor / battery, just a better engineered tee than any existing one on the market today.

We began trying different shapes for the golf tee head, and different materials to make it stronger and more stable. After trying and testing several ideas and designs we finally developed what we believed was a superior and unique product that exceeded our expectations.

With our new design efforts and my sons' engineering expertise, we created a unique golf tee that out-performed conventional tees, proven by testing at the PGA robotics-based golf testing facility in San Diego, California. Our tee provided for directional guidance, more distance in flight off the tee, better controlled back spin, and reduction in left / right directional errors by a significant percentage. The data provided by the independent testing facility and our description of the product awarded us with a patent for the design, and acceptance by the United States Golf Association (USGA) for being in compliance with their detailed rules for golf products. We completed the protection process for our product by adding Trademarks for both the product and our marketing graphics; we were ready to move forward.

Time to name our tee! As a recreational pilot who flew small airplanes, I envisioned a ball leaving the tee and climbing into the sky, then arching back toward the ground for a landing, similar to a small airplane taking off then landing. The name "Flightpath" was born. This was the creation of our new "Flightpath" performance golf tee.

Now, not every attempt to create or reach your American Dream is successful. You may have many setbacks that are out of your control. Just don't give up so easily! My first attempt was successful in creating a wonderful, much-needed product, but I was not able to raise the capital needed to get it to the marketplace. Let me tell you about this particular experience:

Prior to my retirement, I actually invented and held the exclusive patent for "smart gun" technology. I designed an electronic system that required a fingerprint match on a gun before the gun could be fired. This system was ahead of its time and getting venture capital to build the working prototype was next to impossible. My eldest son, Michael, jumped right in and offered to help me develop a business plan. He applied his computer expertise to the product and developed a very comprehensive business plan which included identifying our customer base, and projecting future earnings once we moved the product to the marketplace. He then helped me locate possible venture capitalist groups where we could gain the money necessary to build the necessary prototypes. Michael met with several venture agents and introduced me to several. Unfortunately, there was still a lot of engineering necessary to complete the workable prototypes, and we were unable to secure the money needed. What should we do? Quit? No. Let's put this plan on hold and explore other opportunities. Remember, never give up! You may have to start all over but remember your goal for your American Dream! I began to dream again and that led me to "Flightpath" performance golf tees!.

Whereas I needed approximately $200,000 to fully develop and create the gun prototype, I only needed around $300 to create a working prototype of our performance tee. My son Daniel helped obtain the Computer-Aided Design (CAD) software necessary to create our performance tee prototype on a 3-D printer, and we were on our way! Of course, we had to refine our product and fine-tune it several times, improving it each time until we were finally ready to launch. We tested each version, analyzed the results, and determined whether it was either faulty or simply not up to the standards we were looking for. We continued to modify and strengthen our tee until we were satisfied it was the best design, producing the best performance capable of an entirely new concept.

With a relatively small dollar investment, we opened a Limited Liability Company (LLC) company, then began researching and contracting with manufacturers to create the tee, create the packaging, and assemble the product. My son and I began the start of a wonderful journey, personally visiting golf pro shops located on golf course properties, and golf retail stores where we could sell to them wholesale. What an education – very difficult to get anyone to commit, but a few did. We learned first-hand about marketing, and who our customer base really was. We could have quit at any point along the way, but quitting was not in the plan. Instead, we did a little more research and began contacting golf distribution companies who sold golf products on-line. We were modestly successful with this approach, and we also set up our own website for advertising the product. Additionally, we contracted with Amazon to advertise through them.

This approach met with a little more success, and we were now able to invest in building up our inventory. We also began contacting several of the large established golf companies who manufactured and sold multiple golf products. We attended national golf merchandise shows where the large manufacturers of golf products exhibited their products. We rented a small booth to display our new, unique performance tee, but also visited the display sites of the large golf companies in hopes of licensing or partnering with them. We weren't successful in any partnering, but now our product was on display, and the big companies now knew about us.

We were hoping to partner with one of these companies, but this didn't work out very well. We were too new and too small for them, so we decided to "go it alone", and create our own successful company through extensive marketing strategies. Several of the marketing companies we approached wanted money up front for advertising. But one company, however, had the foresight to see the success our product could create, and offered their marketing services without any up-front investment. They (and we) were so successful in the first year that we decided to partner with them, forming a new

LLC exclusively for our Flightpath tee. The rest is history: In our first year together we achieved approximately $76K in revenue. Our second year returned $670K in revenue, and in our third year we achieved approximately $5.67M in revenue.

Companies that were not interested in meeting with us because we were too small, are now calling us and discussing the possibility of buying our company for significant amounts or partnering with us to greatly expand our business through investments. We are currently considering a very generous offer to buy the entire company and they will continue to sell our product under its' original name.

At this point in time, my American Dream has been achieved! I created something new and unique to the golf industry, I am now financially independent, very happy with what I am doing, and my future looks very bright. It was a long process, but a process of love, spending time with my two sons, and a process of continuous optimism; never giving up, knowing that we would be successful at some point in the plan.

Ok, that's my story ---
Now for your story.

CHAPTER 3:
Your Story:

It doesn't matter what you envision as The American Dream – for you it's unique. It could be designing and creating a new product like I did, it could be starting a business, or it could be earning a post-graduate degree – maybe then going on to become a college professor. Maybe there is a serious medical issue you or someone you care about is suffering from where there is no known cure. You may be the one who comes up with the cure and saves lives as time moves forward.

Your American Dream can be anything you want it to be. It may just be a personal milestone you had always wanted to achieve but never had the time to do it. It may be an irrational idea that comes to you while you sleep, or it may be a very rational desire that you want to achieve. You simply need to identify it, then get busy achieving it!

There may be many roadblocks to face on your way to success; family members and friends may tell you it can't be done; specific rules or laws may need to be navigated. Once you start on your journey, don't quit! I can't say it enough times – Don't quit! For example, if your dream is to earn a post-graduate degree in a new field of study, it may require you to first complete several courses in preparation for your goal. If so, invest the time to complete them. Recognize that it's part of your journey to reach your American Dream and continue moving forward.

I always recommend spending whatever time is necessary to research your idea – your dream. There is so much information available today online with advances in technology that it is worth the time to explore what is out there. This could save countless hours of trial and error by identifying things you need to know to successfully move forward. There may be several obstacles that challenge you, but they can be overcome! You can do this! It's all a part of your journey to success.

CHAPTER 4:
Planning for Success:

Of course, planning is essential for a successful outcome, and we'll cover this in more detail a little later. For now, start by identifying the steps you believe need to be taken, identify the roadblocks (if any) to be overcome, then begin executing your plan. What if your initial plan fails? Do you give up? NO! Remember the story about Thomas Edison who failed in his plan to create an electric light bulb over 10,000 times: when asked about his many failures, he said: "I have not failed, I've just found 10,000 ways that won't work".

Learn from your initial attempts if they don't immediately result in success. Success rarely comes so easily. Recognize what needs to be changed and revise your plans. Just don't quit. (I can't say it enough times). Adjusting, compromising, and sometimes starting over is necessary.

My initial attempts to create something unique had to be abandoned because my "smart gun" design, while capable of being successful, proved to be much too expensive and too far ahead of its' time. I moved to a completely different product, the performance golf tee. Once it was designed and a working prototype was created, we realized there was literally no chance anyone would buy this product and use it when playing golf. Back to the drawing board! Did we quit? No! We adjusted, we compromised, and revised our initial design into a successful working product.

Remember, having to adjust, compromise, redesign or completely re-think your idea is not failure, these are just steps to take in your journey to reach success – to reach your American Dream!

CHAPTER 5:
The "SADEA" planning Process:

Let's now discuss developing a specific plan for your journey to success: The first and most essential step is to specifically identify what you want to accomplish. As I said before, it doesn't matter if your Dream is an irrational idea that comes to you in your sleep, or a rational idea that you have had for some time but. Now that you have a clear understanding of what needs to be done to reach that beautiful American Dream, you can begin the planning process.

There are many ways to plan your journey based on what you intend to accomplish. Don't be afraid to try several possible paths as you develop your strategy. Plan it, try it, then assess your results to determine if you should continue down this path or revise your plan to travel in a modified direction. I personally tried several plans until I found the one that worked best for me and resulted in success.

I suggest a process that I developed a long time ago and have used many times in my life known as "SADEA: Scope, Analyze, Develop, Execute, and Assess".

S: Scope out and identify all the information and data available to help guide you to achieve your plan. There are many sources where you can locate and collect information. Today the computer is a valuable tool for research and information gathering. I made extensive use of the computer before moving forward. A second good source is your local library. Most libraries today are very digitized, so you don't have to sit at a table with a collection of books to review. They give you computer access and everything you want to find is available online at the library site. Also, I suggest you contact and talk to people who may have knowledge of what you are about to go into, as they can provide valuable information and guidance. I was a bit skeptical when I first contacted people in the golf product manufacturing industry, but all were very helpful and willing to offer their advice and recommendations.

<u>A</u>: Analyze the information you gathered and determine the direction your plan is going to take. This is the "big picture" planning of where you are setting your plans and direction. Allow for changes and modifications as this information is analyzed and drawn up. Once you feel comfortable you have a solid view of what you need to do to achieve your American Dream, you're ready for the next step.

<u>D</u>: Develop specific steps to take in your journey to success. Write everything down in the sequence to be followed Be very detailed in this planning step. Plan it as thoroughly as possible. Better to have steps that you will not need, rather than need the steps and not have the information available. Remember, you can always modify and change your steps as you move forward. Once you have it documented and you feel comfortable with your plan, move as quickly as possible to the next step in the process. Don't waste any time procrastinating – It's time to initiate it.

<u>E</u>: Execute your plan; time for action! Do it! This could happen quickly, or it may take an extensive period to complete. Depends on what you are planning to accomplish, and how much time you must devote to it. Don't worry about lost time and possible setbacks. Simply follow the steps in your plan, make adjustments, and continue on until completed.

<u>A</u>: Assess your results. After a short period of time, step back and assess your results. Was it successful? If yes, that's fantastic! If not, which is usually the case the first time around, don't give up, don't quit. Analyze what did not work out as planned, identify any new roadblocks that were not initially known, then modify your plan to correct these issues. Go

back to the SADEA process and begin again with renewed optimism!

This process may require a few iterations (remember Thomas Edison) but persistence and belief in what you want to accomplish will get you to your American Dream!

CHAPTER 6:
In Summary:

IT CAN BE DONE, IT HAS BEEN DONE, YOU CAN DO IT! Just "Dream Big, Never Quit"! Throughout the whole process what drove us to success was <u>persistence</u> and a belief in reaching my American Dream.

If you can dream it, you can create or build it – into a successful self-rewarding result. It's a journey, a process for you to follow. Your first idea may not be the winner, maybe not even the second, but don't quit.

Now get busy – go to sleep and start dreaming: Your American Dream is waiting for you to begin.

CHAPTER 7:
Applying for a Patent.

If you are going to be applying for a patent, know up front that it will cost a little money. You will need drawings of your product that meet the requirements of the patent office. Additionally, the written description of your product and its' functional purpose must meet strict patent requirements.

I've learned over the years that making your own drawings and writing your own descriptions will never meet the strict requirements of the patent office and will be summarily rejected. When I was younger, I loved to "invent" new products, and when I thought I had a great product, I submitted it to the patent office. After multiple rejections I finally did a little research and spoke with a few people involved with the patent process.

What I learned was that the drawings had to meet specific standards, and generally required an engineering firm knowledgeable with the design process to successfully develop presentable drawings of the product. Yes, it does cost a little money, but definitely worth the expense! My first attempt to use an engineering firm for my drawings met with success in the patent office. The second most important lesson I learned was that the description of the product had to follow explicit requirements, and had to satisfy every point in the patent determining process. Who can write such a descriptive paper of a new product? Almost exclusively, it requires a knowledgeable patent attorney, someone well-versed in the requirements set forth by the patent office. This is a bit expensive, but worth every penny!

Doing the drawings and descriptive writings by yourself, then paying the patent submission fee just to have it rejected is much more expensive in the long run. A little research can provide names of firms who specialize in both the drawings and written descriptions, and pricing for this work is generally reasonable. I can't give the name of the company I now use for this purpose, but I am very happy about the success this firm has provided me. Once they prepare the drawings and descriptions they send it to me for my review and make as many changes as necessary without additional cost. Just go online and you will find many companies ready and willing to contract with you for this very important function. They will do the submission, and all you do is sit back and wait for the patent to be approved.

It's a great feeling to be successful with this important step in your desire to be able to reach your American Dream! Your next major step might be to strategically market your product or publish your book if this is what you choose to develop.

CHAPTER 8:
Suggestions for Marketing and Publishing:

1. Marketing.

When we (my son Daniel and I) first started marketing our golf product, we literally went door-to-door attempting to get our product on the shelves of golf pro shops and golf-related retail stores.

We had some minor success but, most importantly, we learned from the experience that this was not our marketplace. These pro shops and retail stores generally selected their products from distributors who had catalogues of golf-related products and visited their customers on an annual basis. We also set up our own website to list our product for sale.

NOTE: There are many companies out there who can assist you in setting up your own professional-looking website for a reasonable cost. Definitely something you want to do!

We also managed to get our product listed for sale on Amazon, which was a bit difficult and not very profitable at the start. We realized from our prior experience that we needed to contract with distributors interested in buying our product wholesale, then advertising it at retail on their own, established websites and catalogues. We were successful in contracting with a couple of distributors and sales were coming along nicely, but this was not enough to help me reach my vision of The American Dream! I needed to get this product advertised nationally and beyond to reach the level of success I dreamed of.

We began researching marketing companies, and found one locally-based company that really liked our product and agreed to take us on as a client with no up-front fees, and with a promise to sell a certain quantity of our products within the first month to show their confidence of successfully marketing our product. They did very well in that first month, and sales continued to grow steadily.

Well, to make this long story short, their sales continued to exceed our expectations and the rest is history! We formed a new LLC with the marketing company and now have distributors world-wide, selling our product in greater numbers than we ever dreamed.

Now, many of the marketing companies that we initially talked with require a set monthly fee to be paid before contracting with us. This is not unusual in the marketing business, but we could not initially afford to risk paying for the service without some guarantee of results. The above-mentioned company we contracted with not only did not require a monthly fee, but they promised to sell a certain quantity of our product to prove their ability to handle our business.

There are many marketing companies and other approaches that you may choose to select based on what your product is and your expectations while searching for the right company or approach. It might take some time and a lot of research to find the best direction to take, but the time spent will be worth it. Remember the overall basic message of this entire book: Don't Quit – Don't Give up! You'll find the right approach to market your product, and your success is just waiting for you as you continue your journey.

2. Publishing:

There are so many options for publishing that a little research on your part will help you find the right process. If you are writing a book of a faith-based nature, there are many faith-based publishers available to take you through the steps. The same goes for children's books, or other specific audience books.

For books of a more general nature, there are publishers who will handle the entire process for you, and there are publishers who offer self-publishing processes if you choose to publish your book yourself. There are also free self-publishing guides available on the internet that will walk you step-by-step of the way.

Two specific examples for self-publishing are:
1. Amazon. Amazon will publish your book, place it for sale, and simply keep a percentage of the profits. You will still maintain 100% ownership and 100% of the royalties. Amazon also offers a ghostwriting service if you choose to have your manuscript reviewed for grammar and suggestions for changes before publishing. Details of the entire process are readily available on the internet by contacting Amazon for the information.

2. Book stores like Barnes & Noble also offer a self-publishing service similar to Amazon. You just need to contact them for the information.

For all publishing processes there are basically five formal steps to keep in mind no matter which process you choose to follow:
1. Consultation
2. Production
3. Promotion
4. Distribution
5. Fulfillment

Plan your publishing process with these five steps in mind and get moving ---your success in reaching your American Dream is just around the corner, waiting for you to finish.

CHAPTER 9:
Success stories of retired persons who reached their American Dream:

1. Cielo F. Cielo moved from Colombia to the United States at an early age, found employment, and married. She had a passion and talent for designing and creating clothes, and upon retiring from her job with a large electronic corporation she decided it was time to follow her dream. She converted one wall of her garage into storage space for all the necessary items for sewing and purchased two commercial sewing machines. She began designing beautiful clothing for her friends and family members, and soon neighbors who saw her creations began asking for her help. Cielo works at her passion several days a week and enjoys other activities in her spare time. Her American Dream has been reached. She remains very happy with her life, and with the enjoyment of fulfilling her dream of expressing her talent and abilities with her family members and friends.

2. Laura W! After retiring, Laura began writing a book that she had in mind for some time. At the age of 65, she decided to go forward with the book. The book was "Little House on the Prairie". Not only was it a "best seller" but it caught the attention of Hollywood and became a television series which ran for many years.

3. Mohr K. Mohr was a combat-tested WWII veteran who was not going to just sit around and do nothing. He continued to stay in shape, and at the ripe old age of 88 made his first successful bungy jump! He continues to bungy jump, and his most recent successful jump was at the age of 96.

4. Harriette T. As a cancer survivor, she was not going to let her medical condition keep her down. She began training for competitive marathon running and completed her first marathon at the age of 76. At the age of 91, she completed her 15th marathon, making her the second-oldest marathon runner in U.S. history.

5. Yuichiro M. He had a dream of doing something spectacular after reaching retirement age. He kept in shape and trained hard, and In 2014 he became the oldest person to reach the top of Mount Everest at the age of 80. He now plans to do it again when he turns 90.

6. Steve M. Steve joined the U.S. Air Force shortly after high school. While serving in the frigid Artic region where temperatures often fell below -40 degrees, Steve dreamed of the tropics where the air and water was warm, and the sandy beaches were very inviting. After leaving the military and working in private industry for many years, Steve retired and moved to sunny South Florida where he bought a kayak and now spends a part of his weekends exploring Southwest Florida's numerous beautiful waterways. An American Dream realized!

7. Gayle W. Gayle has a unique talent for designing and creating jewelry, but as a wife and mother she had little time for her passion. Gayle and her husband Ross both worked full time to provide a good life for their three chil-

dren and fourteen grandchildren. Gayle spent many years working in the hotel service industry, and finally retired to enjoy a more relaxed lifestyle, and to follow her passion for creating her jewelry designs. Gayle and her husband now spend their weekends traveling around the state selling her jewelry creations at craft shows and Farmers Markets. She now enjoys a relaxed life doing what she loves to do. Another American Dream fulfilled.

There are so many more stories of retired people fulfilling their American Dream. Remember, if you want to do it, you can do it! Now get busy and become the next successful story of someone reaching their American Dream.

ACKNOWLEDGMENTS.

I could not have completed this journey without the technical help and support of my two sons, Michael and Daniel. Through the years they both provided invaluable help as I travelled toward fulfilling my American Dream, and again as I began writing this book. Thanks so much!

I also have to thank my wife, Paz, who never complained about the time I spent writing and researching material for this book. She also reviewed the book as it developed and offered suggestions to help make the book more readable.